Love Spells

Mags Pie

Published by Mags Pie, 2023.

LOVE SPELLS

First edition. September 1, 2023.

ISBN: 979-8223931850

Written by Mags Pie.

Table of Contents

Love Spells around the Globe

Mags Pie

Mags Pie

DISCLAIMER

This following non-fictional book is intended to provide information and insights based on the available knowledge and research. This book is designed to present general knowledge and perspectives on the topic. It is not intended to replace professional advice.

Finally, the reader understands that this book is protected by copyright laws and unauthorized reproduction, distribution, or transmission of any part of this book, in any form or by any means, without the prior written permission of the author(s) or publisher, is strictly prohibited. By reading this book, the reader acknowledges and agrees to the terms and conditions stated in this disclaimer.

Preface

The magic melts reality to a plastic consistency in which we can shape it according to our desires and skills, and its most delicious, bewitching and exciting manifestation is love magic.

LOVE SPELLS HAVE EXISTED in all ages, all corners of the world, and all magical traditions. Some sound familiar, others are exotic and daring. Some are poetic; others are the product of quantum psychology. There are three magical states that easily attract love and happiness into our lives. The ability to enter these states and stay there attracts the most incredible events.

THE FIRST MAGICAL STATE is **TRANQUILITY**.

In order to weave and master the threads of creation, the practitioner must be able not just to relax, but to swim in an ocean of peace and pacification. A state of inner peace gives us access to our genius subconscious, to the resources of our creative mind and to our higher self.

THE SECOND MAGICAL state is **ACCEPTANCE**.

By learning to accept, we can get anything we want. In most of the time we live in a state of constant resistance, non-acceptance and rejection. We don't accept our body, we don't accept our weight and we reject our flaws. We resist the events, facts and people in our lives.

Acceptance is not resignation. It is not inertia or passivity. To accept is to act without resistance.

THIS IS A MAGICAL STATE that brings us to the third magical state: **TRUST**.

Learning to trust is not easy. But when we relax, accept ourselves, those around us, and the world, and trust the universe, showing it exactly what we want in our lives and where we want to be, we unlock its magical powers.

MODERN QUANTUM PHYSICS offers a scientific explanation of magic as a tool to control reality. It clearly shows how changing the image of us leads to changes in external circumstances.

EACH PERSON LIVES IN two worlds, the inner and the outer. And although our inner world is wise and profound, most of the time we are simply reacting internally to external circumstances.

BUT SINCE THE OUTER world is constantly shaping our inner reactions, why not assume that the outer world also reacts to the circumstances of our inner world? Let's play this game.

SO, SIMPLY REDUCE YOUR reactions to the outside world and see what happens. Managing external reality always begins with zeroing out reactions to external stimuli and focusing attention on the internal world.

The Key to Happy Life

THE KEY TO A HAPPY life is to easily get what you want and to want what you have. Most people make a mistake: they fixate on a certain object or event in their life, instead of attracting the desired by changing themselves. Through inner work, we change reality much more easily and get the desired result without any problems. This is called reality manipulation, or in other words, magic.

A FEW YEARS AGO I READ the novel *Tuareg* by the Spanish writer Alberto Vázquez Figueroa, a story about one of the last princes of an ancient people who crosses the most sultry, arid and terrifying part of the desert, the white salt core of the Sahara. Wrapped from head to toe in indigo robes, lean, wiry and lithe as a reed, girded with a knife and a battered rifle, he was the epitome of restrained strength. He spoke little, and his face had long since forgotten the taste of a smile.

I AM NOW THE GUIDE preparing to guide you through the fine sands of quantum magic. Therefore, I am obliged to introduce you to the ancient rules of this art:

Don't try to get from others what you don't give yourself.

LOVE IS NOT REACTIVE psychosis. Love is living water. Everything else can be treated.

REALITY AND DESERT sand are similar - they are malleable, but they can overwhelm you.

THE WORLD REFLECTS your inner state. You decide whether you will see a mirage, an oasis or a desert.

IF YOU KEEP EXPECTING a miracle, miracles keep happening. If you constantly expect bad things, bad things always happen. Such is the power of tense expectation.

DO WHATEVER YOU CAN, and leave the rest to fate.

∞

There are no errors. The events we attract into our lives, however unpleasant, are necessary for us to learn what we need to learn. Whatever our next step is, it is necessary to reach the place we have chosen to go.

Richard Bach, *The Bridge Across Forever*

Magic Lore and Traditions

MAGIC IS A PERSIAN word meaning "the art of sorcery," a study of the secret forces in nature that the knower can master and use. In the Middle Ages, they began to divide magic into black and white, according to whether the intended magic was to be achieved through evil or heavenly good spirits.

In the modern world, magic has been relegated to the shelf of cheap high street editions for naive teenage girls and immature housewives. The word *magic* has acquired a negative connotation; it has become a synonym for witchcraft and superstition. And there is nothing surprising in that.

Our modern, high-tech logic, which likes to explain phenomena in purely linear, deterministic causal relationships, has no place for magic.

Magic has been banished from our world and few understand its true nature. Most people perceive it as some dark force that distorts the "laws" governing matter and energy. Popular culture presents magic in exactly this way. But if one turns to antiquity and looks for more reliable sources, such as the ancient Egyptian papyri, the Vedas, the Norse sagas and Irish myths, one finds a completely different reality.

The best definition of magic belongs to Diane Fortune: "the art and science of causing a change in consciousness in accordance with the will."

Magic brings about change by working directly with the conscious, or more precisely the subconscious. From there, its influence spills over subtly and indirectly into the physical world. That is, exactly the opposite of what modern science does. Science causes changes in the physical world according to its "laws".

Magic and science operate in different ways and pursue different goals. That's why wizards don't conduct laboratory experiments and scientists don't chant spells before altars of powerful symbols. The last clause in Diane's definition Fortune, "in accordance with the will," refers to both the wizard's guide and the will of the subject of that spell.

Although there is a perception that magic is universal, there is a huge difference between black and white magic. Magic requires and enforces taking responsibility. Metaphysical knowledge is a source of power and help in the fulfillment of desires, but it should not be used to harm or against the will of others.

The most popular magic is red or love magic. Today it is used by millions of people who want to refresh their love life, regain the passion of their partner, arouse feelings in someone or simply become more attractive.

The three most famous magical traditions in this regard are Arabic magic, Gypsy magic, and voodoo. Other traditions, such as Egyptian, Vedic, and Druidic, also have something to offer in love affairs.

The system of Arabic love magic is based on the making of talismans, amulets, tying knots and invoking jinn. This magical practice originated in Ancient Egypt, the cradle of magic.

Egyptian magic is considered the most powerful, many papyri and wall paintings tell about it, describing supernatural events in the court of the pharaohs and complex rituals performed by the priests and wives of Ra. The Eye of Horus and the Ankh were popular symbols used as protective amulets. In ancient Greece and Rome, talismans were commonly used to ward off evil and bring luck.

Babylon and Persia also made significant contributions to the development of the magical art, and the ancient priests or magicians established the entire system of astrological, numerological and color correspondences and laws.

Having discussed the issue of responsibility, we must also mention the importance of faith. Believing in what you are doing is one of the most important aspects of magic. Skepticism and the voice of the inner critic can sabotage even the most powerful love spell.

∞

The saying "The darkest hour is just before dawn" holds true for magic.

Once you've performed the ritual or spell, the hardest part is waiting.

At this moment, you should "let go" of your desire on the waves of the cosmic ocean and forget about it, or at least trust the magic that it will take care of you in the best way.

Remember that impatience is not a good quality and often leads to loss of faith and self-sabotage.

A major mistake of the novice sorcerer is to expect the effect of the spell the very next day, if not earlier. This is absolutely amazing. Spells draw their power from the universe and its magical powers, so don't try to rush the result.

In some cases, the effect manifests itself within a few days, in others it takes months. It often happens that so much time passes that a person forgets about the cast spell, and the universe seems to be waiting for exactly that to manifest the desire.

Talismans, Amulets, Spells

THE WORD TALISMAN, in Turkish *tilsim* (tilsim) comes from the Arabic *tilasm* (تلسم), which in turn is a derivative of the Greek word *telesma* (τέλεσμ α), which means "to perform a religious ritual." A talisman is an object that possesses certain magical and sacred properties, providing good luck and protection to the wearer. For instance, in Buddhism, amulets called "phylacteries" or "yant" are used to provide protection and blessings. In Islam, amulets called "ta'wiz" or "taweez" are worn for various purposes, such as protection from harm or to bring good fortune.

THE USE OF TALISMANS and amulets is not limited to a specific culture or region. Various cultures worldwide have developed their own unique traditions and practices related to these objects. For example, in West Africa, the "gris-gris" is a type of talisman used for protection or to bring desired outcomes. In Chinese culture, the "fu" character, which means "luck" or "blessing," is often used as a talisman during Lunar New Year celebrations. In the Middle Ages, Christian amulets like the crucifix and Saint Christopher medals were worn for spiritual protection.

ALTHOUGH MOST PEOPLE do not distinguish between an amulet and a talisman, an amulet is an object with natural magical properties, while a talisman must be charged with elemental power and energy by the magician who crafts it.

A TALISMAN IS ALWAYS made with a specific purpose and purpose, while an amulet has a universal application, usually warding off lessons, the evil eye and attracting good luck.

Make It

Personal

SOME IDEAS FOR NATURAL love charms that a person can make and charge themselves are many - a dried rose wrapped in metal foil (metal is the natural element that gives structure), a sprig of rosemary, a piece of jewelry or a piece of amber, an amethyst or emerald for attraction of new love, rose quartz, rhodochrosite or moonstone near the body on a first date to enhance the attractiveness of a first date and jasper or beryl to ignite passion in an existing relationship, a silver heart-shaped pendant, a heart-shaped stone or a piece of dried apple, cut in the shape of a heart.

RUNES ARE A PROVEN helper in love, so use Kano to awaken passion, Berkana to ignite desire and Gebo for a stable relationship. Draw one or three runes on a smooth pebble, piece of wood, or embroider them on your underwear. Seashells are an amulet that inspires love and inspires romantic excitement.

WOMEN THROUGHOUT THE Middle East and Maghreb, from Anatolia to Israel, Egypt and Morocco, wear the Hamsa or the Hand of Fatima. This ancient talisman originates from the ancient cult of the Goddess, symbolizing supreme divine power. Often there is a blue eye in the center of the hand to ward off lessons or a heart to attract love.

IN THE CARIBBEAN, A favorite female talisman is the beautiful filigree heart of Erzulie, written in blue and gold paint. Erzulie is the moody and jealous Haitian goddess of prosperity, abundance, and love, who loves oceanfront rituals with lots of flowers, sweets, and rum.

A POPULAR MALE AMULET in the Mediterranean countries is the red coral pendant, similar to a hot red pepper or phallus, which inspires courage and determination in love affairs, protects against evil forces and preserves harmony in the family.

Love Magic

Love magic aims to attract, "bind" and subjugate the object's passionate desires through magical means rather than through one's own efforts. It is present in all magical traditions and practices, using various spells, dolls and figurines, talismans, amulets, philtres and rituals.

WORLD LITERATURE AND art are saturated with plots and themes related to love magic, from Ancient Greece and Ancient Rome, through the Middle Ages and the Renaissance. These days dozens of movies and novels exploit the golden vein of love charm with the help of ethereal worlds.

INCANTATIONS FOR EROTIC attraction and entrapment exist in the magical tradition of Ancient Hellas, which combines Egyptian and ancient Hebrew elements, documented in ancient texts such as the Greek magical papyri and in archaeological artifacts from the 2nd century BC.

WE FIND MAGICAL LOVE rituals among the Celtic and Germanic peoples. Regardless of tradition, love magic relies primarily on the feminine and feminine qualities: fertility, childbirth, menstruation (obviously closely related to fertility and birth), and the feminine "nature" or "private parts."

A Piece of Advice

B efore diving into the ocean of love spells from different eras, continents and magical traditions, let's clarify a few ground rules.

FIRST, CAST LOVE SPELLS to attract love, to increase your love and erotic potential, but avoid directing the spell at a specific person.

IF YOU ARE OBSESSED with the thought and love of someone to such an extent that you do not want and do not see anyone else, then cast a spell to harmonize and "sweeten" your relationship and relationship, but in no case try to "bend", break or bind the man against his will.

BELIEVE ME, THE KARMIC punishment for such an encroachment on another person's free will is cruel, three times harsher than your deed, and swift.

SECOND, DO NOT RELY on fortune-tellers, psychics and other conniving sorcerers who promise to provide you with the love and fidelity of the man you want for a fee. The power of your desire, attention, energy and sincere love is much stronger than the mercantile machinations of the sorcerers of the "sole trader" type.

REMEMBER, LOVE MAGIC requires an existing relationship on all three levels - sexual, emotional and mental, therefore any promise of "attachment" to a person with whom you do not have a relationship on at least one or two, preferably on all three levels, is empty talk.

AND THIRDLY, BEFORE reaching for love spells, conduct a 21-day personal "cleansing diet", shake off the bitterness and blocks of the past, charge yourself with beauty, joy and energy and bring yourself into an adequate form for love. I wish you success and love!

Useful Props

ROSE QUARTZ IS THE crystal of unconditional love at the same time. This is a gentle energy that will enhance any love spell. You just need to have it by your side.

ATTRACTION OIL CONSISTS of several essential oils and a carrier oil. If you are working on a spell to attract or enhance love, then you can massage your wrists a little and wear it for a few days after you cast the spell. You can also anoint the candle with this oil.

IF YOU HAVE A WAND, then use it for a circle spell. If not, don't worry, you can use your finger. If you are interested in making your own wand, do it.

∞

USE YOUR JOURNAL TO write down your chosen spell. Include your "risk assessment", i.e. why you chose to use this spell. Then write what form your spell takes and the spell cast. Add the date and any subsequent notes.

Time-Tested Love Spells

Make a Wish (Middle East)

IN TURKEY, LEBANON and all over the Balkans, young women believe in the efficacy of tying something to a tree in order to get a husband or have a healthy child.

DATING BACK FROM OTTOMAN times, the treatment of an ill person might consist of writing some powerful quotes on a piece of paper, dissolving the paper in water and having the patient drink it.

Another way was to prepare a shirt, and embroider on it words that were considered protective. Topkapi Palace has a number of such "kaftans" that were to be worn by the sultan to keep him safe, although there is no evidence that this practice worked. People believed it did and that was enough.

IN ISTANBUL, IT USED to be the custom to engage in making spells or having them made. Women wanted to ensure their men didn't stray from home or behave harshly to them. Some men wanted to bind a woman to them and vice versa.

31

OTHERS WANTED TRAVELERS to return safely, to find lost items, to conquer the enemy, to see their future. Even today, practically all Turkish women know how to read the future in a coffee cup.

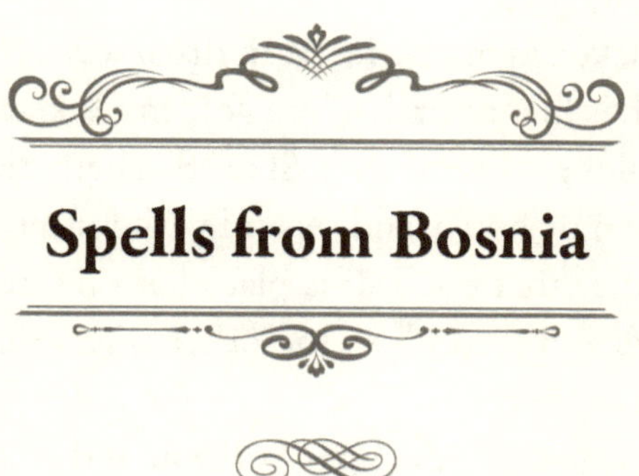

Spells from Bosnia

VARIOUS MAGIC RITUALS aiming to get jinni (spirits/demons) across prove that. One of them is performed by a girl during the night; right before she gets in bed, she knocks the walls saying: "I knocked the wall and 3 jinnis popped out..."

TRADITIONALLY, EVERY witch performs her magic right at the sunset time, although the whole night is adequate for all magic practices, particularly a night before some important holiday when various fortune telling practices are performed too. In that way, a night before Bayram, girls get outside, take a look to the brightest star at the sky and, being very focused, repeat for nine times: "Tell me star, who loves me, tell me is it the one I love too?" Immediately after this they go directly to bed and if they happen to dream about men they love that night; it is a proof that their love is mutual.

THE SPECIAL ATTENTION in love magic Bosnian witches pay to a herb called milogled, commonly known as asarabacca or European wild ginger (asarum europaeum) for which they believe it possesses a power to stimulate erotic desires in a monotonic marriage and to fire up love in the heart of the wanted person.

Milogled is picked up in the forest in ritual way at the sunset time, in a way that an herb is first encircled by a golden necklace and then pulled up from the soil, along with the root. Since this herb mainly has only two leaves, one is coated by honey and second with butter with magic words being chanted. After that one leaf is placed at one side of the entrance door of the house and second on the other side, in order to get loved person passing between them.

The moment beloved person passes through the door; the leaves are to be immediately glued to each other and carried along for some period of time. If this magic is performed for the husband then the mentioned leaves are to be put in his pillow.

A GREAT POWER TO SEDUCE the desired person, according to believes in Bosnia, comes from amulets made by a mullah (Islamic priest). Amulets made for this purpose are normally kept as talismans or burned in fire, beloved person is looked at through them or they are to be buried underneath the beloved person's threshold.

SOMETIMES, AMULET IS burned down and ash is to be poured in a drink or meal of a desired person. It is believed that this is very powerful magic. However, its effects often last for 40 days only after what the magic is to be repeated.

IN LOVE MAGIC, HUMAN secretions (sperm, vaginal secretion) are often used. After sexual intercourse woman picks the sperm of her lower by a kerchief after what she wipes her vagina with it. Then she washes a kerchief in a glass of water and she puts that water in her lover's coffee or soup with magical words being chanted.

APART FROM SPERM, MENSTRUAL blood is also very much in use in the whole of Bosnia. Woman gets menstrual blood fall on the sugar cube (normally 3 drops), and by chanting magic words she puts it in the coffee of the desired man.

ACCORDING TO BELIEFS in Bosnia, woman have got two sorts of blood; one is menstrual blood that will make a desired man passionate and obsessed with her, and second; located in the fingers of a fist, which is used for practicing magic that will make beloved man obey her will and dominated by her.

Binding Spell

Take seven silk threads of varying colors, tie them into seven knots, and then recite the following incantation seven times on each knot:

ANEEF (X2), BISABSAB (x2), Katamtah (x2), Talaflafat (x2), Majanjafat (x2).

Atharvaveda (India)

This is the Ralph T.H. Griffith translation of the Atharvaveda.

The Atharvaveda is a Vedic-era collection of spells, prayers, charms, and hymns. There are prayers to protect crops from lightning and drought, charms against venomous serpents, love spells, healing spells, hundreds of verses, some derived from the Rigveda, all very ancient.

Apsara Love Spell

This is the Apsarases' love-spell, the conquering, resistless ones'.

SEND THE SPELL FORTH, ye Deities! Let him consume with love of me.

I pray, may he remember me, think of me, loving and beloved.

Send forth the spell, ye Deities! Let him consume with love of me. That he may think of me, that I may never, never think of him.

SEND FORTH THE SPELL, ye Deities! Let him consume with love of me.

Madden him, Maruts, madden him. Madden him, madden him, O Air.

Madden him, Agni, madden him. Let him consume with love of me.

Love Drawing Condenser

INGREDIENTS

Small pot or cauldron

Spring water

Pink or red rose petals

8 oz. vodka

Clear glass bowl

A piece of silver

Plastic wrap

Ruby red bottle

Technique

Pour the water into the pot and bring to a boil. Add a handful of rose petals, cover the pot, and turn off the heat. Allow the petals to steep for one hour. Add some vodka to the mixture to preserve it. When the mixture has cooled, pour it into a the bowl. Place the piece of silver in the bottom of the bowl. Place your hands over the bowl and infuse the condenser with your thoughts and desires as you chant:

FROM EARTH TO WATER and river to sea
  The love I desire shall come unto me.
  By power of herb and deep emotion,
  Bring true love and deep devotion.

COVER THE BOWL WITH the plastic wrap and place it in direct moonlight. Allow the condenser about an hour to absorb the power from the moon. Store the condenser in the ruby red bottle, along with the silver. Label and use in love- drawing spells or to dress candles.

Love Potion #9

INGREDIENTS

9 oz. sweet red wine

9 basil leaves

9 red rose petals

9 cloves

9 apple seeds

9 drops vanilla extract

9 drops strawberry juice

1 ginseng root, cut into 9 equal pieces

Technique

By the light of 9 pink votive candles, put these nine ingredients into a cauldron on the 9th hour of the 9th day of the 9th month of they year. Stir the potion 9 times with a wooden spoon, each time recite the following magickal incantation:

Let the one who drinks this wine

Shower me with love divine

Sweet Love Potion Number Nine

Make his/her love forever mine

Bring the mixture to a boil, then reduce the heat and let it simmer for 9 minutes. Remove from heat and allow cooling. Blow 9 times upon the potion; bless it in the names of nine goddesses. Strain through cheesecloth (or coffee filter–it is the 90's thank you). Store in a clean container and refrigerate until you are ready to serve it to the one from whom you desire love and affection.

Do not allow anyone other than your beloved look at, touch or drink the love potion.

WARNING: extremely potent and should be used with caution. Its results can be very intense, long-lasting and difficult to control or reverse.

(Don't direct it or it's your karma!)

Candle Spell for Passion

TO DRAW A PASSIONATE love your way, during a waxing Moon gather two taper candles, one pink and one red, and some red thread and jasmine oil.

Anoint the candles with jasmine oil using your fingertips, then light them while visualizing the flames of passion growing between yourself and new, but yet unknown, love.

Link the candles together by making a figure eight between them with the thread while repeating:

"Flames of passion and seeds of romance grow;
I open my heart to love. Now the one who seeks me shall
come."

For best results, enact the spell on three consecutive nights.

Win Someone's Love

The spell to win the love of the person you love will make your loved one fall deeply and deeply in love with you. This will not be a fleeting infatuation or infatuation, but a true lifelong love.

The ritual stimulates strong, healthy, true love that will connect the couple in a fulfilling relationship, bringing joy and happiness to both parties.

You can use this ritual to achieve true love without harming anyone.

The spell makes you more attractive and reciprocates – a response – your true feelings.

This spell will start a new relationship that will stand the test of time.

Ingredients

1 RED CANDLE
 1 tablespoon lemon zest
 1 tablespoon periwinkle wintergreen
 1 tablespoon of cloves
 Rose oil
 Jasmine incense
 Sheet
 Ballpoint pen
 Matches

TECHNIQUE

Trace a circle with chalk. You can cast a magic circle.

Anoint the candle with the rose oil. Light the red candle. Light the jasmine incense stick from the candle flame.

Focus your attention on your beloved and gather energy to attract him into your life.

Write your name and the name of your loved one on a piece of paper.

Drop 7 drops of wax on both of your names. Add the lemon zest, wintergreen and cloves in that order. Follow with 3 drops of rose oil.

Again, drip 7 drops of wax onto the names.

Fold the sheet 7 times so that the contents remain wrapped inside.

Burn to ashes.

THROW THE ASHES INTO a natural water source (lake, stream, river, sea).

Thank the goddess of water.

Lakshmi Spell

Lakshmi spell that will make your lover adore you

Lakshmi is the Indian goddess of fertility, abundance and a happy love life. You can use her symbols and rituals to awaken the adoration of your beloved.

This love spell will release energies that will create strong feelings of adoration in your lover or any other person you wish to cast this spell on.

The spell has a wonderful side effect - it will make you attract money and success in business, and make you popular in society.

Ingredients
A shared photo of you and your loved one
One dark pink - purple - candle
One blue candle
A soft pink candle
Champagne glass filled with sea water or rosé champagne
Emerald green, gold and blue brocade
A small statue or picture of Lakshmi or a pink lotus

TECHNIQUE
The best time for this spell is on a full or new moon.

ARRANGE THE FOUR CANDLES in a square. Place the statue of Lakshmi or the pink lotus in the center of the quadrant. Prop the photo of you and your loved one onto the lotus or statue. If you use a pink lotus

This spell should be cast on the night of the new moon.

Go to a beach or a large body of water and meditate on the message you want to send to your lost loved one. Find the perfect seashell on the beach. the pictures of the strand of your hair, the sprig of rosemary and the leaf with the two names between the two halves of the shell. Tie it with the red end and drop it into the water with the direction of the seashell to carry your astral message to your loved one.

Some considerations

Black magic can allow you to achieve whatever you desire, but working with dark forces has few dangers as you will never have full control or understanding of these forces.

The consequences of black magic can be unimaginable and terrible, as this type of magic is used to purposefully harm another, but even in cases where you do not intend to cause harm, you can still cause harm unintentionally.

BEFORE YOU CAST A BLACK love spell, you must first ask yourself if you are willing to risk any unintended consequences that might arise from the spell intended to attract the person back to you.

If it is imperative to use black magic, do so only as a last resort. If you have explored all other solutions to the problem and still believe that black magic is the optimal way to make your lover come back to you, then use this spell.

Be sure to perform a spiritual cleansing after the ritual is completed. Whenever you use black magic, be aware that even if you get what you want, it may not be exactly what you expect.

Once you unleash the power of black magic into the world, there is no way to curb, stop or reverse it, so always exercise extreme caution when casting such spells.

Passion Spell

The pleasant moment of sitting in front of the door, me and you.
With two figures and two faces, with one life, me and you.
Joyful and careless, free from distracting myths, me and you.
Me and you, without us, gather because of love.
- Rumi

This is a wonderful ancient and time-tested spell that creates sexual desire and passion between two people and can be done with or without the participation of the object of your desires.

The spell will help ignite the love passion of your beloved, allowing him to immerse himself in thoughts and feelings that he has suppressed, denied or ignored up until this point.

Since ancient times, patchouli has been an incense associated with carnal love and the inflaming of sensual passion, and in tantra it is used for the introductory massage of the bodies of lovers before proceeding to sacred sex. The apple is the symbol of original sin. The blood that flows through the fragrant smoke of the sticks binds you together as a couple.

Ingredients

A pin

An apple

Patchouli essential oil

Technique

Each of you must prick your finger with the pin. The drop of blood should fall on the incense stick. Light it up. pick up the apple and push it through the smoke. Say:

The blood of (his name)

The blood of (your name)

Merge into one.

Push the apple through the smoke two more times, repeating the spell. Cut the apple in half and place it in front of the incense. The spell creates intense passion almost instantly, so be ready!

The benefits of this spell

Use the passion spell to ignite the passion of a real partner or to seduce and attract a new lover. Remember that passion is a beautiful and natural element of life. You can use this spell without any fear that you are manipulating or forcing your partner into something he or she is not really feeling.

The passion spell that aims to ignite erotic desire in your love relationship should be cast when the moon is waxing, and for optimal results during a full moon. Sexual magic is an ancient and powerful practice that allows you to merge your own vision (psychic vision) with the powerful lunar energies that can help you fulfill your desires and make your life better - attract happiness and love in my life.

Tarot Cards Love Spell

Ingredients
     2 pink candles,
Star card
Lovers card
King of cups card

The ritual is performed in the evening, before going to bed.

Cover the table with a red or white tablecloth, arrange the 2 candles and light them. Pick up the Star card and imagine how the thing that holds back your lover disappears. Place the card in front of you.

Take the King of Cups in your hand and imagine that all the good traits of his character, say:

I call on all 4 elements, I call on all good spirits, I call on all the gods of love! Make the path of my beloved smooth and fast so that he becomes mine!

Put the card on the table.

Take the Lovers card, imagine that you are together, say:

I call on love, and it will come, brought by the flame of a candle, wherever it is, whether near or far. My love will come to me, I give love, and I receive love in return. Our love is passionate like a candle flame, our love is strong like fire, our love will last as long as I wish. The ritual is complete. Let it be so!

Leave the cards on the table until the candles burn out.

Sweet Love Spell

SOMETIMES LOVE BECOMES too routine. "I love you" comes out of the mouth in an almost nonsensical way. You know you love each other, but that beautiful sparkle of romance has thinned. What you need is a big dose of sweetness to get you back together.

INGREDIENTS

Sugar and spices, candies and other goodies that "speak" to you...

Technique

ARRANGE THE SWEETS on your altar or magical circle and say:
> *Come see me and my partner, you really should.*
> *Sweeten our love, make it divine.*
> *I love him/her, I love him/her he/she's all mine.*

Keep Love Secret

THERE CAN BE MANY REASONS why you want to keep this relationship a secret, and it would be helpful to work out a variation of a protection spell to shield you from public scrutiny and scrutiny.

KEEP OUR LOVE A SECRET, let no one tell.
No speculation or gossip, quiet as in a well.
Our connection is hidden to everyone.
When we're ready, we confess.

Love Spell with a Photo

HOW TO CHARM THE MAN of your dreams? If you feel like you care about the guy you care about, then you can try simple photo love spells. In this case, you will not need any magical formulations and herbs that are hard to find.

White magic uses the energy of your feelings. To cast a spell, you must focus on the photo of your loved one and say out loud your good intentions. It is important that the words come straight from the heart, so don't overthink what to say.

Love spells with a photograph can also be made in order to strengthen the already existing feeling that led to the union.

INGREDIENTS

    2 pictures: yours and of your partner
    A jar of honey or rose jam
    Some rose oil
    1 red candle
    1 red thread with a needle

TECHNIQUE

FIRST RUB THE CANDLES with the rose oil. Then fold the photos in half so that your images are the image inside.

Sew the edges of the photos with the red thread, then put them in the jar of honey.

PLACE A CANDLE ON THE lid. Light it up all the time representing your happy life.

Love Charm

WHAT TO DO IN A SITUATION where you do not have a photo of a person to whom you feel love? You can cast the "love me" spell at him.

INGREDIENTS

To perform the ritual, you will need:
A round table
A red tablecloth
A red candle
A red rose
Two pins

TECHNIQUE

This spell is very powerful, so in order for everything to work out well, you first need to cleanse your space, for example, using white sage incense. Then, on a covered table, place a candle and stick pins into it: the first right at the base of the wick, and the other a few millimeters below.

It is important that they do not overlap.

Place the roses to the left of the candle. When you light the fuse, don't stop thinking about your loved one. Cast the following spell:

LET YOUR HEART BE LIT like this candle, and let the flame show you its soul.

REPEAT THESE WORDS until the candle burns out to the point where the second pin is.

At the end of this ritual, set the roses on fire.

Slavic Love Spells

THE SLAVS USED SEVERAL ways to attract and keep love. In Russian culture, self-made amulets to attract a loved one played a special role.

Such a magical attribute can be made from three stripes: red, green and white. They are braided into a braid, which is then fixed with wax from a red candle. At the end, a willow branch is attached to the wax.

Slavic magic was so strong that young girls, with the help of certain rites, could find out who would be their husband in the future.

To this end, they covered the table with a white cloth, putting two hats on it: one for themselves, and the second for the future lover.

THEN A MIRROR WAS PLACED in front of the table, the girl stood naked in front of it and focused on her reflection.

IN HER THOUGHTS SHE invited her future husband to dinner, until the figure of her future groom appeared on the surface of the mirror.

Then, she imagined how that magical dinner would go on, the dishes, the phrases, the looks and the attraction between them.

Amen.

Full Moon Love Spell

LOVE SPELLS CAST DURING the full moon also have amazing power.

According to ancient beliefs, this phase has the strongest effect on earthly affairs, because the Silver Month at this time becomes in opposition to the Sun.

DURING THE SPELL, YOU must write down on a piece of paper all the qualities of your ideal man.

THEN FOLD THE LEAF in half, consecrate it with incense and press it to your chest. With your right hand, tear off the petals from the red rose, squeeze them tightly, then start thinking about a happy life side by side with the partner from your dreams.

Put the petals in an envelope, seal it, and make a seal at the junction with a kiss with your lips, painted with red lipstick. Be patient. You will feel the effect of your spell over the next six months.

Conclusion

DEAR READER,

May this tiny book serve as a constant reminder that you deserve honoured and true love. Your heart's desires and your honest intentions matter and your attitude can change the world.

Dare to believe in yourself, embrace your potential, and embark on a journey of self-love, compassion, and personal growth. The path may not always be easy, but with the unwavering conviction that resides within you, you can overcome any obstacle and manifest a life beyond your wildest dreams.

And remember, the world is waiting for you to shine your light and make a difference. Trust in yourself, and let the love journey begin.

Don't miss out!

Visit the website below and you can sign up to receive emails whenever Mags Pie publishes a new book. There's no charge and no obligation.

https://books2read.com/r/B-A-KBUZ-GPPNC

BOOKS 2 READ

Connecting independent readers to independent writers.

Did you love *Love Spells*? Then you should read *Dream Reader*[1] by Mags Pie!

Have you ever wondered what an enigmatic dream is trying to tell you? Dreams have fascinated humanity since time immemorial, captivating our curiosity and igniting our desire to unravel their mysteries.

In this book, we embark on an exploration of the remarkable realm of dreams, delving into the ancient knowledge of their meaning and interpretation, relying on history and psychology to shed light on the significance of over 120 images and scenarios you might see in your night dream.

Drawing upon the wisdom of ancient traditions and the insights gleaned from modern psychology, this book offers practical guidance on how to interpret dreams and harness their transformative power.

1. https://books2read.com/u/497P88

2. https://books2read.com/u/497P88

By understanding the messages your dreams convey, you can unlock hidden truths, gain clarity about your deepest desires, and navigate life's challenges with heightened awareness.

Also by Mags Pie

All About Eggs
Dream Reader
With Knife & Fork Around the Globe
Fin, the Fish of Syllable Sea
Чудесаторът
Love Spells